Original title:
Melon's Dream

Copyright © 2025 Creative Arts Management OÜ
All rights reserved.

Author: Elliot Harrison
ISBN HARDBACK: 978-1-80586-375-5
ISBN PAPERBACK: 978-1-80586-847-7

Sunlit Fantasies

In a garden full of glee,
A fruit danced by the tree.
Wearing shades and a hat,
Sipping juice, how about that?

Bees buzzed with a silly tune,
While frogs croaked under the moon.
A picnic spread in the grass,
Where laughter always comes to pass.

Juicy Daydreams

A slice wore a tiny crown,
Rolling round the sunny town.
Juggling seeds with utmost flair,
Spreading joy without a care.

Sunshine spills like lemonade,
Where every moment's a charade.
Bouncing on a bright pink plate,
Tasting giggles—never late.

Slices of Serenity

Wobbling on a silver tray,
A cheerful friend comes out to play.
Spinning tales in the light,
Wishing on a star, so bright.

With each bite, the world feels light,
Colors dance in pure delight.
Laughter drips like sweet reward,
In this land, we are adored.

The Watercolor Mirage

On a canvas of pastel hues,
Fragrant breezes softly cruise.
Sipping laughter, I can melt,
In this dream, pure joy is felt.

With every splash of color bright,
Surreal shapes come into sight.
A comical twist in every seam,
Wanders through this whimsical dream.

Moments of Rind and Time

In a garden full of cheer,
Round and sweet, the fruit is near,
With a grin that could outshine,
Let the juicy laughter twine.

Chasing seeds like tiny birds,
Hiccuping on silly words,
With each bite, the giggles grow,
A splash of joy in every throw.

Beneath the Canopy of Colors

Underneath the leafy shade,
Bright and bold, the colors played,
A splash of pink in every smile,
Let's enjoy this silly style.

Bouncing like a summer breeze,
Jokes are carried with such ease,
Tasting joy with every slice,
Nature's candy, oh so nice!

Lulling Glistens

Glistening gems in the sun's warm light,
Wobbling around is quite a sight,
With a wiggle, giggle, and a jest,
Let's munch and laugh, we are blessed.

Sipping nectar, giggling loud,
Joyful chatter fills the crowd,
In the tease of flavor's dance,
Who knew fruit could lead to romance?

The Oasis of Flavor

In the heat, a sweet retreat,
Where laughter meets a juicy treat,
Bubbles of joy in every bite,
Let's savor this silly delight.

While daylight winks, we share a grin,
Sliced and served, let the fun begin,
A fruity tale we all will weave,
In this oasis, we won't leave.

Fragrant Fantasies Underneath the Vine

In the garden where giggles grow,
Bright fruits dance with a charming glow.
Bees wear hats, they buzz and swirl,
While ladybugs twirl in a playful whirl.

A rabbit plays chess with a sly old fox,
Counting beans instead of rocks.
All the flavors join in the fun,
As laughter ripples under the sun.

Chasing Shadows at Dusk

As daylight fades and shadows creep,
Mice in tuxedos begin to leap.
With tiny shoes that squeak and squeal,
They race through fields for a grand meal.

The moon is a ball, bright on the rise,
While owls tell jokes in clever disguise.
Fireflies blink like stars at play,
In this whimsical twilight ballet.

Lush Visions Beneath the Canopy

Beneath the leaves, where secrets hide,
A parade of flavors spins with pride.
Tiny ants in a conga line,
March to the beat of a sweet design.

In the midst of petals, laughter erupts,
While frogs in crowns lead joyful cups.
A sprinkle of joy in every bite,
Turns the dusk into sheer delight.

The Ripple of Sun-Kissed Bliss

Sunbeams bubble upon the ground,
With giggles lifting all around.
A dandy dog strolls with flair,
As birds harmonize in the warm air.

In laughter's echo, flavors collide,
While a squirrel juggles nuts with pride.
A splash of humor in every cheer,
Creates a garden filled with pure gear.

Savoring the Golden Hour

In fields of laughter, they roll and trot,
With sun-kissed faces, they tease a lot.
Chasing the shadows, they skip and prance,
Who knew the hour could turn to chance?

Sticky fingers and giggles loud,
Kites in the wind, lost in the cloud.
A slice of sunshine, so sweet and bright,
Melting in joy, a pure delight.

Dewy Midnight Reflections

The stars peek down with a playful wink,
As critters gather for a midnight drink.
A sip of laughter from goblets of light,
Dewdrops sparkle like dreams in the night.

Whispers of mischief fill the cool air,
As shadows dance with a mischievous flair.
Under the moon, secrets softly glow,
Who even knew the grass could flow?

Hues of Lush Abundance

In orchards bursting with colors bright,
Fruits hum a tune in the golden light.
A burst of joy with every bite,
Rainbow treats that spark delight.

The apples chuckle, the pears grin wide,
In this happy harvest, there's nowhere to hide.
A blend of laughter from trees so tall,
Echoes of giggles in nature's sprawl.

Secrets Hidden in Orchard Shadows

Beneath the branches where sunlight fades,
Lies a world of laughter, joy cascades.
Rascally critters with flourish and flair,
Spin tales so funny, you stop and stare.

With rustling leaves, they plot and jest,
A secret club, they're the very best.
In the hush of the orchard, smiles take flight,
As shadows whisper, 'What an odd sight!'

The Color of Dreams

In a field where colors blend,
A purple pickle is my friend.
Jumping high on jelly bean,
Oh, what fun in a fruity scene!

A rainbow laughs in the bright sky,
As carrots dance, oh me, oh my!
Bananas wear the silliest grin,
While the spinach spins round and round, we spin!

Cotton candy clouds float by,
Chasing each other, oh so spry.
A strawberry sings a silly tune,
While night falls softly, like a balloon.

Whimsical hues in every shade,
Jelly spills, and giggles cascade.
In this land of colorful delight,
Every moment feels just right!

Floating Memories

A bubble pops, then drifts away,
With each burst, a chuckle does play.
Banana boats sail on the breeze,
While watermelon seeds float with ease.

A slick slide made of taffy twist,
In this world, who could resist?
The memories glide on cotton fluff,
As we bounce through laughter, never tough.

Sundae swirls in the summer air,
Giggling dandelions dance with flair.
Cherries wink from the treetops high,
Inviting us to jump, oh my!

Every moment a giggling ride,
On this floaty joy, we won't hide.
With laughter echoing far and near,
Every memory brings us cheer!

A Playground of Taste

Swinging high on candy canes,
A burst of laughter, no more reins.
Slides that shine with sweet, bright hue,
In this playground, we jump right through.

Tasting giggles from the air,
Popcorn clouds without a care.
Grapes rolling down a gentle hill,
Chasing them brings the biggest thrill.

Lollipops serve as all our swings,
As chocolate birds dance and sing.
Every flavor surprises and cheers,
Magical moments conquering fears.

In this taste bud land we roam,
Each funny bite feels like home.
Together we savor every grin,
In this playground, fun will never end!

The Harmony of Green

In a patch of green where laughter grows,
Cucumbers waltz in silly bows.
Avocados giggle, ripe with glee,
As we dance around, just you and me.

Frogs on leaves, they leap and cheer,
A lime jingles, "Come over here!"
While peas play music with sweet delight,
Creating rhythms that feel just right.

Zucchini whispers in jovial chats,
Amongst us all, it's where humor sits.
Each leaf giggles at the sun's warm glow,
As we sip on laughter in a flow.

Oh, the harmony of life so green,
Bringing joy in ways unseen.
Every moment, a chuckle we glean,
In this garden, where dreams convene!

A Patch of Serenity

In a garden where fruits play,
A big smile, bright as the day.
The sun giggles, spreading her rays,
Jolly shadows dance in a sway.

Chubby critters strut with glee,
Plump and round as they can be.
They bounce around, oh what a spree,
In this patch, wild and free.

Blossoms whisper sweet secrets,
Winks exchanged as no regret.
Laughter floats on breezy jets,
Here joy blooms, and no one frets.

With each slice of nature's treat,
Life's a banquet, oh so sweet.
Everyone joins in the beat,
In this patch, no room for defeat.

Portraits of Pleasure

Canvas splashed with colors bright,
Each slice painted, pure delight.
A fruit fiesta, what a sight,
Laughter echoes, day and night.

Round and juicy characters play,
In this gallery, they sway.
Chubby faces lead the way,
In each bite, a fun array.

Crimson smiles, a burst of cheer,
Tickled taste buds, pulling near.
Every giggle a souvenir,
In this space, no room for fear.

With juicy joy, let's all partake,
Fun-filled moments, yet no fake.
Raise a toast, let's celebrate,
In this portrait, giggles quake.

Soft as Summer Rain

Pitter-patter on green leaves,
Nature dances, joy believes.
With each droplet, laughter weaves,
A playful tune that never leaves.

The sun peeks from behind clouds,
Tickled fruits join merry crowds.
Bubbles pop, oh, laughter loud,
In this rain, no need for shrouds.

Each splash brings a burst of cheer,
Silly skits that soak us here.
Grins expand from ear to ear,
In this dribble, fun is clear.

So let it rain, let spirits rise,
With each drop, sweet surprise.
Joyful puddles, crazy ties,
In nature's play, our laughter flies.

The Spirit of Freshness

Awake with the morning dew,
Bright and cheery, all things new.
Funky flavors, a vibrant crew,
In this freshness, life's a view.

Round delights on a wooden plate,
Sprightly bites, oh, what a fate!
Ticklish taste buds, can't wait,
In this spirit, joy's our mate.

Bubble giggles, juicy fun,
Chasing shadows, we all run.
Cheerful moments under the sun,
In this world, we've just begun.

So join the dance, sway along,
In this freshness, all belong.
With every bite, we sing our song,
In lively spots, where joy is strong.

Radiance Caught in a Breath

In a garden full of giggles,
A fruit danced with a swirl,
Wobbling under the sun's gaze,
It twirled like a dizzy girl.

A slice of joy fell to the ground,
With a crunch and a squelch!
The laughter rippled all around,
As flavors began to belch!

The bees buzzed with a cheeky tune,
While butterflies played tag,
They feasted on the sweetness,
As they shimmied and wagged!

The juice spilled dreams on the grass,
With giggles that filled the air,
A party thrown by nature herself,
In this whimsical fair!

Flavors of a Forgotten Feast

In a pantry hosting a wild shindig,
Old jars began to sway,
A relic of zest yelled out,
'Come taste my fruity play!'

With raisins in fancy hats,
And nuts plotting their schemes,
A salad of laughter concocted,
Unraveled all those dreams!

Oh, the flavors had a riot,
All jumbled in one pot,
The kitchen echoed with chuckles,
As chaos hit the spot!

Then out came a drippy sponge cake,
With a wink and a squish,
'Remember to savor your life!'
'Let's start with a splish!'

Lush Retreats in Dreamscape

In a meadow of giggles, they roam,
Fruits with hats and sweet allure,
They dance on clouds of cream,
    Enticing all to venture!

With every bounce, a pop was made,
A lemonade waterfall flowed,
Laughter trickled like honey,
As sweet secrets were bestowed!

The sun snoozed; cheeky rays peered,
Through leaves where confetti hung,
While berries held a masquerade,
    In melodies lightly sung.

Flavors twisted in merry spins,
As dreams were piled on plates,
The air filled with fruity jokes,
And smiles that radiated fates!

Taste of Sunlit Journeys

Embarking on a quest so funny,
With snacks that giggled and grinned,
Each nibble a pop of sunshine,
The journey had truly begun!

Through valleys of plump delight,
Each fruit played a jolly role,
The road was a plush, juicy carpet,
Leading straight to the bowl of soul!

Tickled tongues with zesty sparks,
As berries jived with zestful beats,
The paths were paved with sweetness,
In this land of sunny treats!

With every flavor told a tale,
Each laugh a refreshing brew,
A banquet served by whims and wishes,
Forever bright, forever new!

Enchanted Orchard

In a grove where laughter grows,
Fruit giggles, their colors glow,
With dancing leaves that tease the breeze,
And wily winds that slice with ease.

A plump treat with a juicy grin,
Winks at you, come join the spin,
The squirrels wear hats, the bees all hum,
In this place, all joy is fun.

A Tapestry of Colors

Reds and greens in sunlit scenes,
Chasing rainbows, oh, what dreams!
Pumpkin pies and breezy laughs,
Giggling trees in silly graphs.

A purple beast, a joyful sight,
With polka dots that dance in light,
A burst of fun in every round,
Where tastes of joy are truly found.

Garden Whimsy

In a garden where tickles grow,
Worms wear sunglasses, wouldn't you know?
The daisies laugh, the petunias cheer,
As frogs recite their poems near.

A playful breeze with a goofy twist,
Crop circles spun, can't resist,
In this patch, all cares are small,
Join the fun, just plant it all!

The Enigma of Slices

Round and ripe upon a plate,
Slice reveals its funny fate,
Giggling seeds in cheeky rows,
Pointing out their juicy foes.

A pie chart of pure delight,
Bold creations, oh what a sight!
With every slice, a laugh will bloom,
In this world, joy finds room.

The Palette of Bliss

In a garden of giggles, colors collide,
A splash of laughter, where joy can't hide.
Watermelon winks, in hues so bright,
Chasing the sun, till the fall of night.

Bouncing on clouds, with friends all around,
Splashing in puddles, giggles abound.
Paint me in stripes, in zany delight,
Together we dance, under stars' tiny light.

Tranquil Sips

Sipping the sunshine, a frothy delight,
Straws twist and twirl, in the warm, soft light.
Giggles arise, in fruity parade,
As sweetness flows, like a playful cascade.

Chilling on swings, with mischief nearby,
Unexpected splashes, as laughter flies high.
In cups filled with cheer, our spirits unite,
To savor the moments, in pure delight!

A Playful Harvest

Gathering fruits, in capers so grand,
Tickles and chuckles, go hand in hand.
The orchard's alive, with a whimsical sway,
As giggling shapes dance, and prance all day.

Juicy adventures, we pluck from the tree,
A medley of flavor, wild and free.
Life's a sweet joke, with every bite taken,
In the heart of the harvest, no dreams are forsaken.

Daydreaming in Orchard Hues

Clouds fluff like candy, drifting so slow,
In an orchard of laughs, where time does not go.
Daydreams of mischief, ripe with good fun,
As the sun watches over, and all has begun.

Crisp bites of sweetness, with each crazy thought,
Jokes bloom like blossoms, in sunshine caught.
In colors so vibrant, we giggle and sway,
Oh, these orchard hues steal our cares away.

A Garden of Delight

In a patch of green so bright,
Laughter dances in the light.
Giggles sprout from silly seeds,
While carrots try to plant some weeds.

Tomatoes wear their finest hats,
Chasing down the playful rats.
Sunflowers sway with grinning glee,
Waving 'hi' to bumblebees.

Cucumbers join in on the fun,
Telling jokes beneath the sun.
Radishes play peek-a-boo,
While pumpkins dance a jig or two.

A garden filled with quirky cheer,
Where plants and laughter grow each year.
Embrace the joy that nature brings,
In this patch where humor sings.

Fragrant Horizons

Underneath a sky so wide,
Where silly scents and smiles collide.
Lavender hats on dandy sprigs,
Bumblebees don their ballet gigs.

Sneeze of pollen, laughter loud,
A lilac's pirouette makes one proud.
Skipping daisies laugh out loud,
As the wind plays in the crowd.

Scented jokes fill up the air,
Tulips wink with colors rare.
In fragrant fields where giggles bloom,
Cheerful whispers lift the gloom.

A horizon painted with pure glee,
Where dreams collide with jubilee.
Fragrant moments, oh what a thrill,
In the laughter, we find our fill.

Nectar's Embrace

Sweet drops of joy, a sticky mess,
Bees tell stories, no need to guess.
Hummingbirds giggle in a race,
Chasing nectar's warm embrace.

Petals blush in colors bold,
Making sweet secrets to be told.
Buzzing friends share silly tales,
As honey drips from tiny trails.

Butterflies flap with all their might,
In gardens kissed by the soft twilight.
A hive of laughter floats on high,
Underneath the watchful sky.

Nature's nectar, oh what a treat,
In every drop, a funny beat.
Enjoy the sweetness life can bring,
In every laugh, our hearts take wing.

Moonlit Harvest

Under the stars with giggling glee,
The veggies peek, all kinds, you see.
Cabbages roll in a moonlight dance,
While radishes play a game of chance.

Garlic whispers silly rhymes,
As the harvest marks good times.
Potatoes dig themselves up high,
While pumpkins swap jokes on the sly.

Beneath the glow, the shadows play,
Vegetables laugh at end of day.
A harvest blessed with funny cheer,
Filling baskets year after year.

So gather 'round, both old and young,
In this moonlit tale, let laughter be sung.
For every crop that feels so bold,
A funny story yet to be told.

The Taste of Sunshine

In a garden bright and bold,
Laughter's found in every fold.
With colors bright, like painted toys,
Sweetness shared brings endless joys.

Juicy bites and giggles flow,
A sticky slice, a sunny show.
Rolling laughter, oh what fun,
Underneath the warming sun.

Delightful pangs of merry cheer,
A wiggly dance, the end is near.
Sticky fingers, happy feet,
Sunshine fills the town so sweet.

Vibrant Reflections

In a bowl of colors bright,
Slices shimmer, what a sight.
Juicy wonders flip and flop,
In this carnival, we can't stop.

Giggles jump from slice to slice,
What a treat, oh isn't it nice?
Bouncing bits of laughter ring,
Like a jester in the spring.

Squishy bites and silly grins,
Cheerful chaos, laughter wins.
A colorful feast, what a scene,
In this bubble of routine.

The Serenade of Slices

Slicing through the day with glee,
A chorus of joy sings out, 'Whee!'
Twirling treats that run and roll,
Harmony in every bowl.

In fruity fun, we take a chance,
Jumpy bits, we twist and dance.
Laughter bursts like sparkling lights,
Each juicy bite ignites delights.

Strumming jokes and funny quotes,
Slice by slice, the laughter floats.
Every nibble, a playful jest,
In this feast, we are all blessed.

Baskets of Wonder

Filled with colors, baskets sway,
Wonders waiting every day.
Charming shapes and playful hues,
A treasure hunt with funny clues.

Jokes and giggles spilling out,
As we munch, we twist and shout.
Round and round, the fun won't cease,
A joyful feast, a slice of peace.

Baskets tumble, laughter's call,
Rolling joy, we share with all.
Every bite, a dancing song,
In this world, we all belong.

Sweet Simmerings of Summer

Beneath the sun, so hot and bright,
Fruit floats by on a picnic sight.
Giggles burst like juicy bites,
Laughter spills, oh what a night!

Chasing bees around the fields,
Sticky fingers, nature yields.
With every slice, the joy reveals,
A world where childhood never shields.

Sipping juice, the drips will race,
Running wild, a silly chase.
Every bite, a happy face,
Melting worries, gone without a trace.

Whispering Waves of Juicy Delight

The beach is lined with sweet surprises,
A summer treat that tantalizes.
With every wave, the happy cries,
Of fruity snacks and sunlit skies.

Sandy toes and spills galore,
Finding treasures, what's in store?
Watermelons roll, they implore,
To take a bite and beg for more.

Seagulls laugh as they take flight,
While we munch in pure delight.
Each juicy wedge, a pure invite,
To giggle 'til the stars are bright.

The Sunlit Serenade of Orchard Dreams

Lying down on grass so green,
Fruity notes form a funny scene.
Nature's jester, round and keen,
Whispers sweet things, ever serene.

The fruit parade, they march with glee,
Hats of leaves, what a sight to see!
Orchards sing in harmony,
As juicy joys just want to be.

Dancing shadows in the sun,
With silly laughs, we'll never shun.
The day is bright, the fun's begun,
In orchard dreams, we are all one.

A Slice of Paradise

In gardens lush, the colors pop,
With every slice, the joy won't stop.
Laughter echoes, a fruity flop,
As memories like bubbles, drop.

Juicy treats on the picnic spread,
With every bite, silly things said.
Under the sky, where light is bred,
We dance and play, no tears to shed.

A sunny slice, a perfect chance,
To twirl and spin, a merry dance.
With every laugh, our spirits prance,
In paradise, we'll take a stance.

The Nectar of Nightfall

In twilight's glow, a slice divine,
A fruity moon with stars that shine.
Giggles rise from shadows spry,
As flavors dance and laughter flies.

A jester pranced with seeds galore,
Tasting joy, then shouting more!
With every bite, a chuckle heard,
Sipping sweetness like a bird.

Laughter ripens on the vine,
A comedy of fruit, so fine.
As night unfolds its purple cloak,
Funny whispers, laughter spoke.

In every seed, a tale anew,
A banquet fit for a silly crew.
Beneath the stars, we feast and cheer,
Fruitful joy is always near.

Fruitful Whispers

In gardens bright, where laughter grows,
A patch of giggles in the rows.
Whispers waft on gentle breeze,
Teasing flavors, sweet as cheese.

A fruit parade with skirts so bright,
Danced through dusk, a silly sight.
Each berry chuckles, ripe and bold,
Telling secrets, tales retold.

With every slice, a joke appeared,
A fruit punchline that we cheered.
Lemon's zesty grin so wide,
Tickled taste buds, joy supplied.

Together we share this tasty land,
Slicing laughter with a hand.
In the orchard, giggles gleam,
A fruity life, a funny dream.

Patterns of Juicy Light

In the sun, they shimmer bright,
Colors dance, a pure delight.
Patterns woven with every hue,
Funny shapes that tickle you.

Round and plump, they play the fool,
Rolling 'round like kids at school.
Banana peels in playful toss,
Who knew fruit could be such gloss?

Straws like swords, we duel with cheer,
Slice a giggle, gather near.
Each juicy bite, a burst of joy,
Silly games for every girl and boy.

In this patch of fruity glee,
Every laugh's a jubilee.
Patterns of light, they gleefully show,
The comedy of fruit, in a glow.

The Essence of a Summer's Day

On summer's lap, the flavors bloom,
Juicy joy dispels the gloom.
A fruity feast with giggles grand,
We nibble happiness so unplanned.

Sunshine spills like lemonade,
Each bite, a wink, with laughter made.
Pineapples wearing crowns of cheer,
Invite us all to gather near.

Watermelon slices, big and bright,
Splatter smiles with each delight.
The seeds fly like confetti spry,
As warmth and chuckles fill the sky.

In every corner, joy's embrace,
Fruity chaos, a sunny race.
This essence of our sunny play,
Forever etched in bright array.

The Tapestry of Summer's Offerings

Beneath the sun, a feast so grand,
Fruits align like a band.
Watermelon winks from afar,
Chasing dreams in a jar.

In laughter's tune, the bees agree,
Buzzing 'round in summer's spree.
A slice of joy, fresh, and sweet,
Tickles our toes, a tasty treat.

Jellyfish skydive, oh what a sight,
While children giggle, hearts take flight.
A canvas painted with vibrant hue,
Where shadows dance, and jests ensue.

With every bite, a smile shines,
Juicy tales and happy lines.
In this tapestry, fun's the theme,
We weave our happiness, a shared dream.

A Garden Where Wishes Bloom

In the garden where laughter grows,
Wishes bloom like a row of prose.
Cucumbers gossip, carrots cheer,
Winking stars, we pull them near.

Sunlight trickles, giggles play,
Veggies dress up for the day.
Radishes dressed in spun gold lace,
Join in the fun at a sprout-filled race.

With fairy wings, chives wave hello,
As tomatoes blush with a sunlit glow.
In this plot of playful delight,
Every sprout brings joy and light.

We harvest smiles, giggles galore,
Open the gate, let's explore!
In this garden, we share our bliss,
With each pluck, a whimsical kiss.

Sipping Sunbeams on the Porch

On the porch, the sunbeams pour,
In funny cups, we beg for more.
Lemonade flows, stories collide,
As laughter dances, there's no need to hide.

Flip-flops squeak on the wooden floor,
Every sip opens up a door.
Sunshine swirls in our glasses bright,
Creating giggles that take to flight.

Chasing shadows with a silly grin,
Tickling the breeze, we dive right in.
Talking to clouds, we giggle and sway,
In this sunny haven, we play all day.

With punchy jokes and bright balloons,
We toast to our afternoon tunes.
Sipping sunbeams, laughter's boon,
In this sweet moment, we choose the tune.

The Green Mosaic of Forgotten Days

In a patchwork quilt of grassy dreams,
Old memories bubble like playful streams.
Pineapple hats and grape-stained cheeks,
Whimsy and laughter are all that speaks.

Collecting wishes in leafy bowls,
Juggling fruits like playful souls.
The ants join in, a tiny parade,
Marching boldly where shadows fade.

With every nibble, joy rewinds,
Echoes of laughter dance and binds.
Stacks of fun piled high in sight,
A green mosaic shining bright.

As twilight whispers, the fun remains,
In the garden of laughter, where joy gains.
We paint our days in hues of cheer,
Collecting moments we hold dear.

The Glistening Muse

In a garden where laughter grows,
Lively fruits do the silliest pose.
A round delight with a coat so green,
Whispers secrets but won't be seen.

Under the sun, they giggle and roll,
One takes a dive, what a jolly stroll!
With seeds of mischief, they plot and scheme,
Creating chaos like a vivid dream.

The juice cascades, a slippery foe,
Chasing the ants in a funny show.
Bouncing and bouncing, it's quite the jest,
A fruit parade, what a silly fest!

With every slice, the laughter erupts,
A comedy of errors as joy constructs.
What's serious? Not a thing in sight,
In this world of whimsy, all feels right.

A Symphony of Rind

Oh, the orchestra of taste so sweet,
Each bite a note, a fruity treat.
Strings of flavor, a piquant tease,
Melodies burst like a soft summer breeze.

Round and jolly, it rolls away,
Humming a tune of the splashing play.
With each juicy chord and sticky laugh,
Twists and turns in a juicy path.

The rind like armor, silly and stout,
Makes silly faces, there's no doubt.
Dancing on tables, the laughter rings,
A fruity concert; oh, how it sings!

As ribbons of zest twirl through the air,
Bees and bugs join the fun with flair.
A lighthearted vibe that tickles the mind,
In this fruity concert, joy we find.

Liquid Joy

A splashy pool of sunny delight,
Sipped through straws on a warm summer night.
Dripping with laughter, the sweetness arrives,
Each gulp a giggle; oh, how it thrives!

In cups that wobble and jostle about,
Spills turn to smiles; there's no need to pout.
A carousel of colors, all bright and bold,
Liquid sunshine in tall cups of gold.

Friends gather 'round, stories unfold,
Sipping the sweetness, a joy to behold.
Stumbling on words, laughter sets free,
As we share in the chorus of sweet jubilee.

What a concoction of pure silly art,
In each tiny bubble, we find the heart.
With flavors of joy on this merry ride,
Liquid happiness, our laughter's guide.

Slice of Solitude

In a quiet corner, a slice sits alone,
Soft whispers of sweetness behind its throne.
Peeling back layers, it laughs in delight,
A solo adventure that feels just right.

The fork winks slyly, oh what a tease,
Carving out giggles with effortless ease.
Staring in wonder at the vibrant hue,
Each bite a secret that feels brand new.

A cozy moment, just me and my treat,
Time tickles lightly, nothing beats this feat.
The world melts away in every sweet bite,
A solo escape bathed in soft light.

With juices flowing, I savor the throng,
A whimsical lullaby, nature's sweet song.
Here in my solitude, giggles abound,
In each joyful morsel, pure bliss is found.

Dreaming in Shades of Summer

In a world made of sprinkles and sun,
Fruit hats parade, oh what fun!
All the colors dance on ice,
A summer smile, just so nice.

Wobbling jellybeans in a row,
Cactus cats put on a show.
Lemonade rivers flow like streams,
Making a splash in our wild dreams.

Flying frisbees, fruity and bright,
Catching clouds, delight in flight.
Giggles bubble like fizzy drinks,
In the heat, all the laughter clinks.

Cloud candy floating, sweet and light,
Chasing shadows in golden light.
Tickles from the wind that sweeps,
In this place, we laugh till we weep.

The Flavorful Journey

A gumball ship sails the sky,
Tasting rainbows as we fly.
Sprinkled cupcakes lining the way,
In frosting fields, we long to play.

Banana boats drift on the breeze,
With chocolate sails that tease and please.
Caramel rivers swirl and twirl,
Every flavor makes our heads whirl.

Bouncing berries in a race,
Marshmallow clouds, a fluffy place.
Giggles bounce like jellybeans,
In this land of silly scenes.

Cotton candy hugs all around,
In this dreamland, joy is found.
Laughter echoes, sweet and clear,
On this journey, we persevere.

Sweet Remnants of Day

The sun dips low with a wink,
As fruity dreams begin to link.
Skies painted with orange delight,
Stars pop up like cheery bites.

Ice cream castles melt away,
Leaving giggles in playful sway.
Chocolate trails lead us around,
In this land where joys abound.

Frothy waves of soda cheer,
Tickling toes, bringing us near.
Whipped cream clouds flirt overhead,
In a world where fun is fed.

Nighttime whispers, candy bright,
Fireflies dance, a playful sight.
In sweet remnants, we find our way,
Laughing as we greet the day.

Rustic Whispers

In a garden where pickles grow,
Jokes are told by a dancing crow.
Tomatoes giggle as they sway,
In rustic whispers, come what may.

Old windmills spin with a song,
Cheering us on as we stroll along.
A parade of veggies on a spree,
Turning farm fields into glee.

Crickets chirp in silly beats,
Bouncing radishes on their feet.
Corncob hats that twirl and spin,
In this fun, we all dive in.

Sunset paints, a jolly hue,
With laughter that feels fresh and new.
In this earthy, humorous scheme,
We frolic deep in a hearty dream.

Juicy Reveries of a Lazy Afternoon

In the sun, a fruit does gleam,
Rolling gently, life a dream.
Sipping juice, both cold and sweet,
With sticky fingers, summer's treat.

Lazily I sprawl on grass,
Watching clouds like sweetened mass.
A splash of color, bright and bold,
Makes the afternoon pure gold.

Bouncing thoughts on bouncing ants,
Imagining small, fruity dances.
Each giggle with a splash of zest,
In this dreamy, funny fest.

Laughter bubbles, juice does spill,
Happiness is time stood still.
Fruity friends come out to play,
In this whimsy of the day.

The Sweetness of Time Unfolded.

Tick-tock goes the silly clock,
But not for me—I wear no smock.
Just fruity thoughts and giggles shared,
In this moment, nothing's spared.

Slicing time like watermelon,
With laughter that is quite compelling.
Juice dribbles down my chin so bright,
As I revel in the silly sight.

Daydreams sprout like vines they say,
With each thought that leads astray.
Joking 'bout what fruits can do,
Like flying through the sky so blue.

A sweetness that is rarely found,
When fruity joy spins round and round.
Come join me in this light-hearted game,
Where time is sweet, but never tame.

Whispers of Sweetness

Blushing cheeks of fruity glow,
Whispers float, as soft winds blow.
A funny thought, a giggle here,
Every slice brings more good cheer.

Underneath a shady tree,
Fruity secrets shared with glee.
What if grapes could crack a joke?
I laugh until I almost choke.

With laughter, I take a bite,
Each flavor bursts—oh, what a delight!
Juicy tales of every kind,
Make this moment one of a kind.

Nature's candy, bright and bold,
Life's little tales waiting to be told.
In this sweet and silly space,
Happiness is every trace.

The Fruitful Reverie

In a grove of laughs and cheer,
Fruity wonders draw me near.
Bouncing fruits and silly sounds,
Add to joy that knows no bounds.

A whimsical dance, let's give it a whirl,
As oranges twist, we giggle and twirl.
In this dream where sweetness reigns,
Nothing dulls, nor any pains.

Bananas split into a laugh,
Pineapples wear a silly scarf.
With every bite, the humor grows,
In this land where laughter flows.

So come along, let's share the fun,
With every fruit, we've surely won.
In this fruitful, joyous spree,
Silliness is the key, you see!

The Blooming Mirage

In a garden bright with glee,
Fruit hats dance upon each tree.
Squirrels sing with silly flair,
Wearing shoes, they prance in air.

Glowing sun, a cheeky tease,
Tickles bees with gentle breeze.
Flowers giggle, petals sway,
Chasing clouds that drift away.

A rabbit leaps with joyful cheer,
Balancing a hat of beer.
Ducks in bow ties waddle near,
Their silly quacks, a tune so clear.

In this place, all quirks align,
Wonders sprout, like wacky vines.
Where laughter blooms and shadows gleam,
Life unfolds a comic theme.

Lush Illusions

A pineapple rides on a bike,
Winking at the passing pike.
Kites made of lettuce fly,
As crisp leaves wave and wave goodbye.

Juicy whispers fill the air,
Cantaloupes with fashion flair.
Tiptoeing on clouds of fluff,
Every moment's just enough.

A pickle plays the saxophone,
While carrots dance, they've found their tone.
The tofu sways with a grand ol' grace,
All rooted in this lively place.

With every sip of sunshine's beam,
The world transforms into a dream.
Full of giggles and fruity fun,
Where life's a dance, and everyone's won.

Ripened Reverberations

Bouncing berries roll around,
In a kingdom, laughter's crowned.
Cherries chase a bouncing ball,
Giggling, they could never fall.

Tomatoes juggle in the shade,
Wearing shades, they form a parade.
Radishes stand, all prim and neat,
While peas provide a marching beat.

In bright lands where mischief plays,
Strawberry knights win the day.
With armor made from cupcake cream,
They conquer all in this sweet dream.

Each fruity turn, a chuckle found,
In a land where joys abound.
As laughter flows in every stream,
Join the fun, embrace the gleam.

The Essence of Bliss

Beneath the beams, the pumpkins twirl,
With giggles that make the dancers swirl.
Carrot cakes leap with glee,
A comical sight for all to see.

Fruits in hats join in a jest,
Making merry as they zest.
Limes and lemons share a wink,
In their punches, fizzy drink.

A peach declared, 'I'm royalty!'
As kiwi chants its loyalty.
Together they sing, oh what a sight,
In this world of pure delight.

Under stars, the laughter soars,
Chasing away all boring chores.
Where joy and whimsy take a fling,
In this realm, who needs a king?

Elysian Encounters

In the orchard, shadows play,
Funny fruits in bright array.
A giggling gourd rolled down the hill,
Chasing a pear with joyful thrill.

The apple danced a wobbly jig,
While oranges sang, big and sprig.
Bananas slipped, but never fell,
In this fruity, silly shell.

A watermelon shared a pun so sweet,
With a rhyme that's hard to beat.
Laughter echoed in the breeze,
As grapes grew bold and teased the trees.

Underneath the sun's warm gleam,
Every fruit had quite the dream.
In this land of laughter, bright,
Silly songs take joyful flight.

Harvest of Dreams

In fields where the whimsical grow,
A pumpkin whispered soft and slow.
Carrots giggled, all aglow,
Sharing secrets only they know.

A salad toss would make you swoon,
Dancing radishes in the moon.
Cucumbers wore their finest hats,
While garlic shared its crazy chats.

The corn stood tall with pockets full,
Tickling beans in a playful pull.
Lettuce laughed in leafy shades,
Creating jokes in green cascades.

As harvest time brought joy anew,
Fruits and veggies played a view.
In this land of fun and cheer,
Every plant's a comedian here.

Ethereal Juices

In a world where drinks can sing,
Lemonade told tales of spring.
A smoothie joined with flair and style,
Making everyone stop and smile.

Pineapple wearing shades so bright,
Shared a laugh that felt just right.
With laughter bubbling, sweet and clear,
The punchline danced to bring good cheer.

Grapefruit joked, with zest and zing,
About the highs of citrus bling.
While watermelon splashed around,
In joy that simply knows no bounds.

A toast to drinks that charm the crowd,
With laughter that is always loud.
Sip and giggle, that's the theme,
In this land of fruity dreams.

Wandering Through Sweetness

Through orchards where absurdity grows,
With gummy bears and fruity shows.
A jellybean walked with a swagger,
While chocolate danced, a happy dagger.

Marshmallows floated in witty loops,
As cupcakes piped their silly whoops.
A donut tossed sprinkles with flair,
Whirls of laughter filled the air.

In candy lands where sweetness reigns,
Gummy worms played silly games.
With taffy pulling jokes so loud,
The lollipops formed a merry crowd.

So wander through this candy tale,
Where sweetness always laughs and prevails.
In sugary dreams, be carefree,
And let the fun take you to glee.

Beneath the Weight of Sweetness

In the garden where fruits collide,
A curious squash does try to hide.
Underneath a leaf, so plush,
With dreams of a berry, it makes a rush.

Jesters of the vine all around,
With whispers of sugar, they spin and bound.
A watermelon's giggle, so loud and clear,
While zucchini dances with ungraceful cheer.

The silly cucumbers laugh and roll,
Competing for laughter, that's their goal.
As the sun beams down with a glimmer of glee,
Nature's pranksters, wild and free.

So raise your glass to the garden's jest,
In the patch of delights, we are truly blessed.
With every chuckle echoing, it seems,
We find our joy in the silliest dreams.

Echoes of a Sun-Drenched Eden

In the orchard full of zesty plays,
Where fruits engage in sunlit rays.
A tomato juggles, just for fun,
While peppers giggle, basking in sun.

The bananas drift, doing the twist,
A dancing party that can't be missed.
With oranges spinning in a funny race,
Citrus laughter lights up the place.

The nectarines whisper, sharing a tale,
About a melon who once set sail.
But tides of joy carried it high,
To frolic with clouds in a peachy sky.

So here's to the harvest of humorous cheer,
In this Eden where laughter draws near.
When fruit meets sunshine, it's the perfect scheme,
To dance and to sing, and to live in a dream.

The Lullaby of Ripened Juices

As twilight falls on the orchard bright,
Fruits gather close for a jubilee night.
With sweet melodies on the soft breeze,
   They hum together under the trees.

A blueberry strums on a tiny lute,
While strawberries sway in a fruity suit.
In this chorus of colors, the giggles resound,
As the peaches spin round, whirling 'bout sound.

The grapes start to chuckle, plucked with delight,
Juicy secrets shared in the cool of the night.
While cherries giggle, rolled up in a ball,
This zesty lullaby enchants us all.

So close your eyes and join the tune,
In the field of nectar, beneath the moon.
In this world of sweetness, let laughter bloom,
Where dreams are ripe and joy finds room.

Vibrant Echoes of Nature's Bounty

In the fields where the colors explode,
Laughter and freshness equally flowed.
The carrots boisterously sprout from the ground,
While radishes giggle in stems all around.

With sunshine playing peek-a-boo,
The peas crack jokes, they're a lively crew.
A pumpkin rolls past with a gleeful shout,
Inviting the squash to join in the rout.

Zesty cabbages puff in comedic pose,
In this orchestra of vegetables, joy simply grows.
As harvest time brings a festival cheer,
Nature's bounty laughs, spreading good cheer.

So toast to the garden, a whimsical place,
Where every crop dances, each with their grace.
In the vibrant echoes where veggies rival,
We find our delight in nature's spiral.

Under the Canopy of Dreams

Beneath a sky so green and bright,
A fruit parade takes off in flight.
With giggles loud and laughter grand,
We dance around in fruit-filled land.

A bouncing ball of juicy cheer,
Hiccups burst, oh, what a year!
We slide on peels, we spin and glide,
In a rainbow ride, we joyfully bide.

With every crunch, a burst of fun,
We race the breeze, we dash and run.
A family of flavors, sweet and bold,
In this whimsical world, we unfold.

Laughter echoes, the sun's embrace,
In this silly, fruity place.
Dreams float high, like kites in the air,
Under the canopy, let's laugh and share.

Vivid Reflections

In a pond of punchy hues,
A splash of joy, it's what we choose.
This world of wobbles and giggly glints,
Gives our silly minds a joyful rinse.

Paddling on boats of jelly smiles,
We drift along for miles and miles.
Each ripple tells a joke or two,
In vibrant tales of red and blue.

With each reflection, we take a peek,
At funny faces, tongues that squeak.
Oh, how we laugh at silly sights,
In our vivid world, joy ignites.

Bouncing around, we skip and twirl,
With laughter bursts, we whirl and swirl.
In this colorful spree, let's gleefully beam,
Sailing high in our fruity dream.

A Cascade of Flavor

Waters splash with colors bright,
A flavor rush that feels just right.
In the splash zone of tasty cheer,
We swim with joy, our hearts sincere.

Tidal waves of giggles flow,
Tickling toes in a fruity show.
As waves crash with bubbly might,
We dive into joy, what a delight!

The fountain flows with zesty fun,
Melodies of laughter, we've just begun.
With every sip, our spirits soar,
A cascade of flavor, forever more.

Sticky fingers and laughter loud,
We revel together, feeling proud.
In this wild wave, let's splash and gleam,
In a joyful torrent of a tasty theme.

Seeds of Imagination

In gardens hidden, fun takes root,
Sprouting laughter, oh what a hoot!
Each tiny seed, a story told,
Of playful dreams and joys of old.

We plant our wishes in rows so neat,
In patches bright where giggles meet.
As sun beams down on our silly plot,
We dance with glee, tied up in knots.

Rainbows blossom where dreams are sown,
In a world where we can roam.
With silly hats and shuffling feet,
We cultivate joy, and it's so sweet!

So gather 'round, let laughter reign,
In this whimsical garden, we'll entertain.
Growing together, wild and free,
In a patch of dreams, just you and me.

The Dance of Petal and Leaf

In the garden where giggles grow,
Petals twirl with a leaf in tow.
They glide on air, with whispers sweet,
A waltz of colors, a playful feat.

Sunlight chuckles on the ground,
As blossoms leap, joy knows no bound.
A daisy spins, a tulip sways,
In this dance, time slips away.

Bumblebees join with a buzz so fine,
Their rhythm a tune, oh how they shine!
With every step, laughter sprouts,
Nature's party, there's no doubt.

So join the dance, oh do not delay,
Let your worries simply sway.
For in this grove, all hearts will beam,
As petals and leaves share a dream.

In the Embrace of Harvest

In fields of gold, the fruits appear,
Squash and vine whisper in cheer.
Carrots giggle, pumpkins roar,
As baskets fill with nature's score.

The corn does sway, a silly jig,
While veggies hum, in zest they dig.
Ants in a line wear tiny hats,
All join in fun, oh imagine that!

With every pluck, a story spins,
Of silly times, and goofy grins.
The air is thick with laughter's scent,
In every harvest, joy is bent.

So gather 'round this merry feast,
Where every crunch brings laughter's least.
In every bite, a giggle hides,
In the embrace where fun abides.

Serene Whispers on the Breeze

As breezes dance and tickle trees,
Whispers float, carried with ease.
Sweet giggles ride on every gust,
Making branches sway, it's a must!

Clouds chuckle in the summer sky,
As they drift by with a wink and sigh.
The sun plays peek-a-boo with leaves,
In this world, humor never grieves.

With every breeze, a secret's shared,
Nature's joke, oh how we've fared!
Flowers lean in, ears perked high,
Listening close, they can't deny!

So let your heart feel the caress,
Of nature's laughs, in every mess.
In serene whispers, life's a jest,
In the breeze, we find our rest.

Twilight Over the Orchards

As twilight blushes, fruits start to grin,
Apples converse, and pears chime in.
The stars peek down, a playful crew,
Illuminating fruits with a sparkly hue.

Moonlight plays hide and seek with pears,
While crickets provide the music's airs.
A raspberry giggles, caught in delight,
In orchards where flavors take flight.

The breeze tells tales of a day well lived,
Of silly moments and joy it gives.
Beneath the twinkling, a party starts,
With nature's laughter, it warms our hearts.

So come, dear friends, let laughter thrive,
In twilight's embrace, feel so alive.
For in these orchards, fun shines bright,
With every wink of the moonlight.

www.ingramcontent.com/pod-product-compliance
Lightning Source LLC
Chambersburg PA
CBHW062111280426
43661CB00086B/451